W9-AWH-220

Wild Cats

Written by Alice Leonhardt

STECK-VAUGHN
ELEMENTARY · SECONDARY · ADULT · LIBRARY

A Harcourt Classroom Education Company

www.steck-vaughn.com

Contents

Chapter 1

What Is a Wild Cat?

The largest one weighs more than 600 pounds (270 kilograms). Some can roar. All can purr. They have roamed the earth for 10 million years. They are the amazing wild cats!

What are wild cats? They are relatives of the common house cat. The house cat is just one **species**, or kind, of cat. It is tame. The other 34 cat species are wild.

Wild cats can be divided into two groups— those that can roar and those that cannot. The ones that can roar are often called the big cats.

All wild cats have a bone at the bottom of their tongue. In the big cats, part of the bone is **flexible**, so it can move back and forth. The flexible bone helps big cats roar. The lion, tiger, leopard, and jaguar can roar. They are the big cats.

In the other wild cats, the bone at the bottom of the tongue is hard, so they cannot roar. The bobcat cannot roar. Neither can the mountain lion.

All wild cats can purr. The big cats can only purr when they **exhale**, or breathe out. The others can also purr when they inhale. Nobody, not even scientists, knows for sure just *how* cats purr, though.

A male lion's roar can travel more than 5 miles (8 kilometers).

Wild cats are more alike than different. For instance, they are all **predators**. They kill and eat other animals. Their skeletons look alike, too. Even experts have trouble telling a tiger skeleton from a lion skeleton. A cat's skeleton has 40 more bones than a human skeleton. The complex skeleton helps cats twist and turn as they chase their prey.

All wild cats also have powerful jaws. One bite will usually kill their prey. The jagged front teeth tear off chunks of meat. The tongue has tiny spikes to help scrape the meat off bones.

Its long tail helps the cheetah keep its balance.

Wild cats have eyes made for hunting. Their eyes sit on the sides of their head, so the cats can almost see behind themselves. Wild cats also have **keen** eyesight. Even from far away, they can spot the flick of a deer's tail. Most wild cats hunt in dim light.

A wild cat's pupils widen to let in light.

All wild cats have whiskers on each side of their face. They use their whiskers like fingertips. The whiskers help them find their way through a dark, dense jungle or forest.

Wild cats' cup-shaped ears are able to pick up sounds as soft as the flutter of a wing. Wild cats can also turn their ears to hear a noise behind them. They can hear many high sounds that a human cannot.

Inside a wild cat's paws lie long claws. When wild cats walk, the claws **retract** into pockets in the paws. When the cats hunt, the claws spring out to help grab the prey. Once wild cats catch their prey, the animal almost never escapes.

Wild cats use their claws to climb trees.

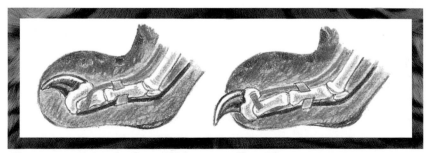

Claws retract when a wild cat walks. They retract to stay sharp and to help the wild cat walk quietly.

Chapter 2

Lions

*L*ate in the afternoon, a lioness sneaks through the tall grass of central Africa. Her golden coat makes her hard to see. Smelling the big cat, a herd of zebras trot nervously around a water hole. The zebras snort. The lioness creeps into view.

The zebras turn and run. Suddenly four more lionesses charge from their hiding places in the brush. The zebras are trapped!

Lions are the only big cats that live and hunt in groups, which are called **prides**. After the lionesses have killed their prey, the pride will feast on it. First, the male lion with its shaggy mane will eat. The females and cubs follow.

A pride has several lionesses. They live in the pride their whole life. Usually 2 to 6 adult males live in the pride. They stay in it for several years or until other males chase them away.

Lion cubs are born with spots that fade away over time.

The members of a pride get along peacefully most of the time. The females even care for each other's cubs. At dinnertime though, lions have terrible manners. They growl, hiss, fight, and steal food. One reason why lions fight during a meal is that they must eat a lot. An adult lion may eat 80 pounds (36 kilograms) of meat at just one meal. That's more than 300 hamburgers!

Adult lions are among the few wild cats that have no spots or stripes. Their dull brown color helps them hide in the dry grass of the wide, open plains. Most lions live in Africa. Some live in a special park in India.

The male lion is known as the king of beasts because he is so big and mighty. His thick mane also makes him look like a proud king. A male lion may weigh as much as 550 pounds (250 kilograms). He protects the pride.

Lions are also called the laziest beasts in Africa. After lions have gorged on a kill, they may sleep for almost a whole day and night. They may not hunt again for a week.

Chapter 3 — Tigers

The tiger creeps silently through the dark forest. Its yellow eyes gleam. Up ahead in a clearing, a wild pig roots in the dirt. The tiger freezes.

The pig looks up and sees the tiger. The tiger springs. With a squeal, the pig scrambles into the trees. The tiger chases the pig but loses it in the bushes. The tiger moans in frustration.

Hot and tired, the tiger heads for the river nearby. When it reaches the shore, it jumps into the water and swims. The water helps clean the tiger's fur and helps the tiger cool down. Soon it must hunt again.

Tigers are the largest members of the cat family. They are so powerful that they can leap 15 feet (5 meters) in the air. They are so strong that a single tiger can knock down a water buffalo that weighs 900 pounds (405 kilograms).

As strong as they are, tigers can only run fast for short distances. Their prey often gets away. Sometimes a tiger must hunt day and night. It may have to chase 15 to 20 animals before it catches one for a meal.

Adult tigers like to live and hunt alone, but when they meet other tigers, they are friendly. Sometimes several tigers share a kill.

The Bengal tiger lives in India.

Like lions, tigers are big eaters. A tiger must eat about 70 large animals a year in order to survive. At one meal a hungry tiger may eat almost twice as much as a lion eats!

Female tigers have 1 to 6 cubs.

If a tiger kills a big animal, it will usually eat some of it and then bury the rest to hide it. The tiger will come back later to eat the buried animal for another meal.

Female tigers are excellent mothers. When a mother returns from hunting, she greets her cubs with a puffing sound. Her cubs grunt, snort, and squeal back. To help keep her cubs safe, a mother will stay with them for 2 years.

Tigers live in Asia. Most live in or near India. They can live in almost any **climate**, so they are found in hot jungles and snowy mountains. Tigers don't go into open country, as lions do. They prefer to be in the shadows.

Each tiger has its own pattern of stripes. Stripes above a tiger's eyes are like a human's fingerprints. No two people have the same fingerprints. No two tigers have the same pattern of stripes on their face.

Siberian tigers are the largest tigers. Some males weigh more than 600 pounds (270 kilograms). Because Siberian tigers live in cold, snowy areas, they are lighter in color than other kinds of tigers and have thick fur.

Sumatran tigers are the smallest of the tigers. They weigh about half as much as Siberian tigers. Because Sumatran tigers live in the hot jungle, their coat is thin. Sumatran tigers are bright orange. Their stripes are spaced close together.

Chapter 4 — Leopards

The female leopard stands over her fresh kill. She sniffs the air, smelling a band of hyenas. She knows they can steal the gazelle from her, and she needs the food for her cubs.

Quickly she grabs the gazelle by the neck. She drags it to a tree. Holding the gazelle in her jaws, she climbs the trunk to the top limbs. She lays the gazelle between two branches. Then she hurries back to the cave where her two cubs are hidden.

"Auu," she calls to her cubs. They follow her to the tree. They scamper up the trunk and start to fight over the food. Gently the mother bites their necks and pulls them apart.

Leopards are the third-largest cats. They are graceful, cunning, and amazingly strong. They hunt and kill monkeys, gazelles, and snakes. They even kill big African porcupines that have very long quills. A leopard can carry a dead animal that weighs 150 pounds (68 kilograms) up a tree.

Black leopards are sometimes called panthers.

Most leopards have beautiful tan coats dotted with black spots. Their coloring helps them blend with the sunlight and shadows. On a leopard's back and sides, the spots form circles called **rosettes**. Sometimes a litter of cubs will have an all-black leopard. The black coat makes the black spots hard to see. But the spots are there.

Leopards roam the mountains, jungles, and deserts of Africa and Asia. Each leopard has its own area called a **home range**. Leopards scratch the bark of trees and spray a **scent** to mark their home range. They also roar loudly to warn other leopards to stay away from their **territory**.

Like tigers, leopards live and hunt alone.

Chapter 5 Jaguars

The jaguar hears the bark of the hounds. He races through the Arizona canyon, finally spotting a tall tree. Swiftly he climbs the tree and hides in the dense branches. Minutes later three hounds bound under the tree. They leap in the air, barking loudly. Two hunters run to the tree and call to the dogs.

The men look up into the branches. When they see the jaguar, they whistle in surprise. Instead of shooting, the hunters take several photos. Then they call to the hounds and leave. The jaguar is safe.

Jaguars are usually found in Mexico, Central America, and South America. They have been spotted in Arizona and New Mexico. They are the only big cats found in the United States.

Jaguars are stockier than their leopard cousins. They have thick necks and short legs. For their size, they have the strongest jaws of all the big cats. The name *jaguar* comes from *yaguara*, a South American Indian word that means "the beast that kills its prey with one bound."

Many jaguars live in the forests of Central America.

Jaguars like water and will dive into a river to catch a turtle. Jaguars have even been known to swim across a river with a dead horse in their mouth!

Like leopards, jaguars have beautiful spotted coats. But unlike leopards, jaguars often have a solid black or brown dot inside the rosette. Black jaguars also have spots, but they are hard to see.

Jaguars can roar loudly. Some South American Indians believe that the jaguar's roar is the sound of thunder before a rain.

Jaguars are very good swimmers.

Chapter 6 — Cheetahs

Hidden in the golden grass, the cheetah waits. In the distance an antelope grazes on the African plain. The cheetah lowers its head. It moves closer, its eyes fixed on the antelope. It holds its long tail high. The white tuft of hair at the end of its tail is the only thing that seems to move as it sneaks through the grass.

The cheetah springs into action. A blur of motion, it races toward the antelope. The antelope sees it, turns, and runs. But it is too late. The cheetah is so swift that it catches up to the antelope in seconds. The chase is over.

Cheetahs are the fastest animals on land. They can reach speeds greater than 60 miles (97 kilometers) an hour. That's much faster than a racehorse!

Cheetahs have long legs, small heads, and long bodies. They have deep chests with powerful lungs and hearts. When they run, their flexible spine pushes them forward like a spring. Because they can bound 33 feet (10 meters) in one step, they have the longest stride among cats.

Cheetahs are fast, but they can only run at top speed for short distances. Then they get tired.

Cheetahs are built for speed.

They have to stop and catch their breath. Many times their prey gets away.

Cheetahs are unusual cats. They cannot roar, so they are not big cats. They are not like the other wild cats, either. Many scientists put cheetahs in a group by themselves.

In many ways cheetahs are like dogs. Instead of slowly **stalking** their prey, they chase it openly. They also hunt during the day. Like some hunting dogs, they use sight instead of smell to find their prey. Their eyesight is so keen that they can see 3 miles (5 kilometers) away.

Cheetahs are the only cats that cannot fully retract their claws. Their claws are dull too, just as dog claws are. The dull claws help cheetahs run fast, but they also make it hard for cheetahs to climb.

Cheetahs are easily tamed. Like dogs, tamed cheetahs love affection and will fetch thrown balls. Long ago cheetahs were trained as hunters. Some say that one ruler owned 1000 hunting cheetahs.

Cheetahs, jaguars, and leopards all have spots. Their coats look alike, but they are different.

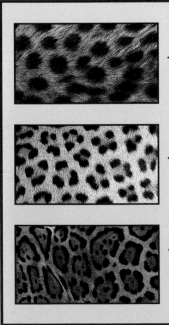

The cheetah has plain spots.

The leopard's spots form rosettes.

The jaguar has one or more spots inside each rosette.

Chapter 7 More Wild Cats

The wild cats that cannot roar make up a big group. About 30 different species belong to this group. These wild cats live on every continent except Australia and Antarctica. Some live in the dry desert. Some live in the snowy mountains. Many are small. In fact, small wild cats are found in more places than any other group of mammals.

Many of the wild cats that cannot roar are not well known. They usually live deep in forests and jungles away from people. Some are so hard to find that even scientists know very little about them.

Mountain Lions

Mountain lions are the largest wild cats that cannot roar. They are also called cougars, pumas, and even panthers. An adult may weigh more than 200 pounds (90 kilograms). Mountain lions live in North America, Central America, and South America.

Mountain lions are good rock climbers.

Mountain lions have small lungs, and they tire easily. Healthy deer can run fast for miles, so mountain lions must sneak up on them. Mountain lions also catch weak deer.

Mountain lions can jump as high as a 2-story house and leap as far as 40 feet (12 meters). Sometimes they drop down onto the backs of deer. They also leap from rock to rock to chase jackrabbits.

Rusty-Spotted Cats

Rusty-spotted cats are the smallest of the wild cats. Three rusty-spotted cats weigh only as much as one house cat. Rusty-spotted cats live in many areas of India. They hunt small birds and mammals and spend a lot of time in the trees. Many of their habits remain a mystery.

The rusty-spotted cat gets its name from the markings on its coat.

Margays spend most of their life in the treetops.

Margays are great tree-climbers. They have flexible feet that hold on to branches like hands. They also have long tails to help them balance on tree limbs. Margays can hang upside down by one paw. They can even dash headfirst down a tree trunk like a squirrel.

Margays are a little bigger than house cats. Males weigh about 9 pounds (4 kilograms). They have beautiful tan fur with both stripes and spots. Margays live in the forests and jungles of Central America and South America. As they scamper in the treetops, they are almost impossible to see.

Bobcats look like large house cats. They like to live alone. They spray their territories to warn other bobcats to stay away. If bobcats meet, they sometimes fight.

Bobcats get their name from their short tail. It looks as if it was cut short, or "bobbed." Bobcats usually have brown fur spotted with grey. The tail has black tips and 4 or 5 dark rings.

Bobcats live in southern Canada, the United States, and Mexico. They are found in mountains, forests, deserts, and swamps.

Bobcats have tufts of fur on their ears.

Fishing cats never stray far from water.

As you can guess, fishing cats love to fish. They will sit for hours on logs sticking out over the swamp. If fish swim by, the cats snag them with their claws. They flip the fish into the air and onto land. If the fishing cats miss, they dive into the water and grab the fish in their jaws. Fishing cats also like to eat snakes and snails.

Fishing cats have gray fur with small brown or black spots. They have 2 stripes that run from their forehead to their neck. They weigh about 25 pounds (11 kilograms) and live in Asia.

Servals

Servals (SUHR vahlz) live in Africa and are called giraffe cats because of their long neck and legs. They also have huge ears that help them locate their main prey—rats. They peer above the high grass, listening. When they hear a soft rustle, they creep silently through the grass. Their hearing is so sharp that they can hear rats that live underground. Servals dig in the ground, then snag the rats with their long toes and claws.

Servals can run fast enough to kill small antelope. They climb well enough to hunt birds. They even wade in water to catch frogs and fish. Servals weigh 20 to 40 pounds (9 to 18 kilograms). They sleep during the day and hunt at night.

Like margays, servals have both stripes and spots.

 Caracals

Caracals (KAR ah kalz) are known for their hunting skills. They can jump high enough to swat a bird off a tree branch. They are so fast that they can catch a gazelle.

Unlike many other wild cats, caracals are easily tamed. In India they were trained to hunt birds and rabbits. People held contests to see how many birds a tame caracal could catch in one leap.

Caracals are tan with no spots. The word *caracal* means "black ears" in Turkish. The name comes from the long black tufts of fur on their ears.

Caracals hunt in open, dry areas and deserts. Their short hair keeps them cool. They can go for a long time without water.

Like bobcats, caracals have tufts of fur on their ears.

Chapter 8

Wild Cats in Danger

Many species of wild cats are endangered. Many are killed. Some are killed by hunters and trappers for their soft, beautiful fur. Others are hunted by farmers and ranchers to keep them away from sheep and cattle. They are killed by cars on the highways. Wild cats are even killed for their bones and their meat.

Wild cats are also losing their home. Every year there are more people on the earth. More and more forests, grasslands, and jungles are turned into farms, roads, cities, and homes. There are fewer places for wild cats to live. There are fewer places for them to hunt.

The Siberian tiger, the snow leopard, and the Florida panther are all in serious danger of becoming **extinct**.

Once there were 8 types of tigers. Now 3 of those types have died out. The Balinese tiger, the Javan tiger, and the Caspian tiger are all gone. There aren't even any photos of the Balinese tiger. You can only see it in drawings.

All tigers are endangered. Scientists think that there are only about 10,000 tigers left in the wild. Of these, the Siberian tiger is very rare. Scientists think there are less than 500 in the wild. One day we may see these magnificent animals only in zoos.

The Siberian tiger is the largest species of tiger.

A long time ago, Florida panthers roamed all over the southeastern United States. They are cousins of the mountain lion. They have the same light brown color, but their hair is shorter. Their tail is crooked, and they have a swirl of hair in the middle of the back. Their paws are slightly smaller than mountain lions', and their legs are longer.

By the 1950s Florida panthers were almost hunted to extinction. In 1967 they were listed as endangered. Today only 30 to 40 can be found, and those are only in parks at the southern tip of Florida.

The Florida panther looks much like a mountain lion.

Snow leopards live high in the mountains in central Asia. They are the best jumpers in the cat family. They can leap more than 50 feet (15 meters) as they travel from ridge to ridge. Their tail is as long as their body. It helps them balance along narrow ledges.

In the winter, snow leopards grow long, thick coats. The outer hairs are as long as a person's finger. The woolly underhair traps heat. Layers of hair on the leopards' huge paws keep these wild cats from sinking when they walk in the snow.

Snow leopards are so rare that no one knows how many there are in the wild. Scientists guess that there may be only about 1000 left.

The snow leopard has been hunted for its beautiful fur.

Many people in many countries are trying to help wild cats. For example, people in India and Nepal have set up **reserves** for tigers. People cannot hunt tigers on reserves. They can shoot pictures of them instead. Other countries have passed laws against hunting and trapping many of the wild cats.

African animal reserves help protect cheetahs.

Lions, tigers, leopards, and jaguars are also found in zoos. Many live in **habitats** instead of cages. Zoo scientists can study the big cats to find ways to help them in the wild. Scientists hope to find ways to keep them from becoming extinct.

Many wild cats will not be as lucky as the big cats. Several species, such as the rusty-spotted cat, are found in only a few zoos. They will soon die out. In the wild they are so hard to find and study that scientists know little about them. If they become extinct in the wild, people will never see them again.

Many zoos build habitats for the big cats.

Glossary

climate the usual weather of a place

exhale to breathe out

extinct no longer living

flexible easily bent; not stiff

habitat an area like an animal's home in the wild

home range the area that an animal lives in

keen sharp

predator an animal that hunts other animals

pride a group of lions

reserve a huge park set aside for animals

retract to draw in

rosette a cluster of spots that looks like a rose

scent a smell

species a group of animals or plants that have the same characteristics

stalk to chase without being seen or heard

territory the area that an animal lives in and often defends from other animals

Index